Em

Publishing

Watch for More Titles
from Ramona Davis

and *Empower Publishing*

He Speaks

in

Quiet Times

By

Ramona Davis

Empower Publishing
Winston-Salem

Empower

Publishing

Empower Publishing
PO Box 26701
Winston-Salem, NC 27114

The opinions expressed in this work are entirely the opinions of the author and do not represent the opinions or thoughts of the publisher. The author has represented and warranted all ownership and/or legal right to publish all the materials in this book.

First Empower Publishing Books edition published February, 2021. Empower Publishing, Feather Pen, and all production design are trademarks.
Cover photo by Ramona Davis
Cover design by Pan Morelli

Scripture quotations marked ESV are from the ESV@ Bible (The Holy Bible, English Standard Version@), copyright 2001 by Crossway Bibles, a publishing ministry of Good News Publishers. Scripture quotations marked NIV are taken from the Holy Bible, New International Version@, NIV@. Copyright 1973, 1978, 1984, 2011 by Biblica, Inc.™ Used by permission of Zondervan. Scripture quotations marked (NLT) are taken from the Holy Bible, New Living Translation, copyright ©1996, 2004, 2015 by Tyndale House Foundation. Used by permission of Tyndale House Publishers. Scripture taken from the New king James Version@. Copyright 1982 by Thomas Nelson. Used by permission.

Manufactured in the United States of America
ISBN 978-1-63066-516-6

This book is dedicated to the glory of God and all who long to draw closer to Him.

Thank you Pastor Clay Olsen for your clearly written steps to salvation.

Special thanks to all of you who shared your hearts and stories.

Thank you sweet prayer partners for joining in this book by faithfully praying for all who will read it. I love you.

—Ramona Davis

Introduction
God is Love

To fall in *love*
with God is the
greatest romance;
to *seek Him*
the greatest adventure;
to *find Him*,
the greatest human
achievement.

—St. Augustine

Do you know God's deep love for you?

God's love for us is often described as lovingkindness, unbreakable loyalty and mercy. God's love is covenant love. The Hebrew word for God's love is *Hesed.* It pictures the love of our Father God as steadfast, ever-faithful, relentless, constantly-pursuing, lavish, extravagant, unrestrained and furious. Through Jesus Christ, *Hesed* is perfectly defined. He is love.

The more we know and experience the vast dimensions of Christ's love, the more there is to know and experience. We can never get to the end of understanding His love for us but it should be something we constantly pursue.

The Apostle Paul prayed "that Christ will be more and more at home in your hearts as you trust in Him. May your roots go down deep into the soil of God's marvelous love, and may you have the power to understand, as all God's people should, how wide, how long, how high, and how deep His love really is. May you experience the love of Christ, though it is so great you will never fully understand it. Then you will be filled with the fullness of life and power that comes from God." (Ephesians 3:17-19 NLT)

It is 2021, unprecedented! Political upheaval, race relations, and all the effects of the Coronavirus have all left us disgusted, shocked and horrified with feelings of helplessness, fear and anguish. Worry and anxiety are at an all-time high. People desire truth, bright hope, strong faith and deep abiding joy but many are overwhelmed with despair, questions, discouragement and depression.

When we pass through seasons of doubt and confusion, when our world is turned upside down, when all our dreams come crashing to the ground, God's love and His promises remain steadfast and true. God promises to care for and protect those whom He has redeemed. He wants to reshape our wrong thinking with His Truth.

The Bible tells us that the greatest commandment given is to love God with all our hearts, souls, minds and strength and to love others. (Matthew 22:37) We can't love Him like that if we don't get to know Him through regular, quiet time with Him.

You have been prayed for long before you picked up this book. If you have yet to set aside quality quiet time with Jesus, may you be encouraged to start. If you already have quiet time, may God's Word and the experiences of those found in this book, motivate you to breathe new life into your quiet time and never give up this important appointment.

But before you continue, I have **the** most important question to ask you...Do you have a personal relationship with Jesus Christ? If not, please don't go another day without Him. Now more than ever you need Him. I pray you will continue reading the steps to salvation written by Pastor Clay Olsen of Emerald Isle Chapel by the Sea and make that decision today.

"How Can I Be Saved?

"For He says, "In the time of My favor I heard you, and in the day of salvation I helped you. I tell you, now is the time of God's favor, now is the day of salvation." 2 Corinthians 6:2 ESV
God's Message:
There is only one way to heaven and eternal life with Him. *"Jesus answered and said to him, "Truly, truly, I say to you, unless one is born again he cannot see the kingdom of God."* John 3:3 ESV
Man's Problem:
Man is unfit for heaven because of sin and he is destined for eternal death and separation from God *"for all have sinned and fall short of the glory of God,"* Romans 3:23 *"For the wages of sin is death, but the free gift of God is eternal life in Christ Jesus our Lord."* Romans 6:23 ESV
God's Desire:
That all man would repent of their sin and be saved. *"The Lord is not slow about His promise, as some count slowness, but is patient toward you, not wishing for any to perish but for all to come to repentance."* 2 Peter 3:9 ESV

God's Solution:

God's sent His only begotten Son to pay the death penalty sentence for our sin, by living a life without sin and dying in our place. *"He made Him who knew no sin to be sin on our behalf, so that we might become the righteousness of God in Him."* 2 Corinthians 5:21 ESV

God's Call:

God is always there calling for sinners to come home. "Behold, I stand at the door and knock; if anyone hears My voice and opens the door, I will come in to him and will dine with him, and he with Me." Revelation3:20 ESV

Your Response:

Behold today is the day of salvation. In repentant faith, turn yourself over to Jesus Christ today and receive His pardon and His righteousness. You can use this prayer to "call upon the Name of the Lord."

Dear Lord Jesus, I know my sins have separated me from You. I know that I need Your forgiveness to cover the penalty of my sins and Your righteousness in order to enter the Kingdom of Heaven. I now repent of my sins and turn my life over to You, Lord Jesus. I do believe that You earned my salvation for me; through dying for my sins in your perfect sacrifice on the cross, and through living on my behalf, a perfect life of obedience and righteousness. I trust in you alone to save me, and I am willing to follow You as Lord of my life. Thank You for granting me forgiveness and a new birth into spiritual life, united with You for eternity. I pray this in Your Name, Jesus. Amen.

If you prayed this prayer, please tell me or a fellow Christian as a way to publicly confess Christ and a way for others to rejoice with you. It is important that you find a good Christian church, a body of believers, to serve with and grow with. These will be your friends for eternity.

Now that you are a born again child of God, a Christian, your first work of faith is to seek out a body of Christians, a local church, to serve and grown in. Equally important, you will want to be baptized, as your first work of faith, publicly demonstrating the private confession of your belief in Jesus. And that is what baptism is, a picture of your death (to your sin nature) and resurrection (new life) with Christ. Make sure the church you attend adheres to the essential uncompromising truths that your new life in Christ rests upon … in the non-essentials liberty and in all things love."

Chapter One
A Lukewarm Heart

"I know all the things you do, that you are neither hot nor cold. I wish that you were one or the other! But since you are like lukewarm water, neither hot nor cold, I will spit you out of my mouth!" Revelation 3:15-16 NLT

My friends buzzed about the women's conference we had just attended while I quietly watched the scenery race by the van window. Like the scenery, a thousand thoughts raced through my mind. They came so rapidly I couldn't examine any one of them for long. There seemed to be a specific purpose for my being at the conference, but what was it? The speakers were great. The music and worship were awesome. But the "Ah-ha" moment I anticipated never came. Not while I was there anyway. Nothing about the weekend stood out.

Silently I questioned the Lord without really expecting an answer. "Why did you bring me to this place? I know there is a reason. What is it?" I was stunned at His immediate and simple reply which I heard from the depths of my being, "Ramona, I'm so tired of you being lukewarm." His answer was filled with love and compassion but that hot truth stabbed down deep in my heart and seared a permanent mark there.

He captivated my heart when I was 13 walking home alone from school. I felt a holy presence envelop me. Instinctively I knew it was Jesus seeking my heart. His presence was strong and His love so persuasive, that my young heart melted. There alone on a peaceful road in North Carolina I asked Jesus to forgive me of my sins and save me. I gave Him all of my heart never thinking anything would come between us.

I wish I could say that I lived my life for Him after that, but

I didn't. I made many poor choices and many mistakes. Without strong Christian guidance, my young, insecure heart was attracted to and prone to follow "friends" with strong personalities. Unfortunately, they were not interested in the things of God. They led and I willingly followed. During these many years, I could hear the still small voice of conviction but I regularly put my fingers in my ears to drown out the whisper. I rebelliously continued on my own way.

My life spiraled until I hit rock bottom. I vividly remember the day I bolted for the door. I was headed on foot for somewhere I just didn't know where. My footsteps turned into a full run. I just kept running. Even now I can hear the blaring car horns. I wasn't on a suicide mission. I just didn't care that they had to dodge me on that blacktop road. I ended up in a church yard under a big oak tree and I fell to my knees because I had nowhere else to go. I cried out to God from the depths of my gut. I don't remember all of that prayer, so much of it was from a wordless place. It was as if my soul heaved. It threw up everything in an unfamiliar, honest prayer. After a while, I rose to my feet with a strange kind of peace.

Although, it didn't happen overnight, God, in His mercy, was answering the raw prayer spoken in desperation under that big oak tree. God stirred my heart in all areas of my life. I had been climbing a corporate ladder only to discover more stress and pressure with each rung. I questioned the value of the work which seemed so hollow. I longed for personal fulfillment. Soon an opportunity to work with children with disabilities in a public school system came my way. Twenty years of service and a deep cut in salary was a small price to pay. I took the job. In serving these special children I experienced blessings of satisfaction and profound joy.

I began to search for this same gratification in other areas of my life. The rituals and illusion of personal interaction at the church I was attending, left me disappointed week after week. I just kept going because that's what Christians do, they go to church. My older son, Dale was 16 and had frequently attended

a church with his close friend, Greg. Dale and Greg met at preschool and had been fast friends since they were two years old. Greg's family were pillars in this church and I was grateful for their influence on my son. I had just begun to attend this church a few months before the women's conference.

The church sponsored a "Friend Day" in which attenders were asked to bring a friend. My son invited me to be his guest. I went. During the service, I could feel the presence of the Holy Spirit and something so real, refreshing and different from the pulpit. It was the Word of God being preached in truth and in love by pastors who were authentic and transparent with their own struggles that drew me in. The people were real and loving and after I attended the women's conference, this new church was vital to my spiritual growth.

There was no miraculous experience until **now**. In that van, it seemed Jesus was sitting beside me showing me that my relationship with Him had grown cold and He was tired of it! He made my hot and cold relationship with Him painstakingly obvious. Convicted, I clearly saw how I ran to Him in desperation when I needed Him to clean up a mess I had made but easily ignored Him when I wanted to satisfy my own desires and will. Of course I prayed, sometimes. I reflected on God's goodness, sometimes. I read the Bible, sometimes. I tried hard not to lie or gossip. I didn't steal or commit murder. I went to church but it seemed most of the sermons were for someone else and they were never there.

As the spirit of the Living God met with me on the road back home from that conference, there was a powerful awakening in my heart much like the day on that quiet road when Jesus first spoke to me. God's love was just as profound and His message just as clear. I had enough of Jesus to get to Heaven, but I needed more of Him to become the person He desired me to be. It was time for a change. Suddenly, I could relate to Saul, who had come face to face with God on the road to Damascus. (Acts 9) He was never the same after his encounter with God. Neither could I remain the same.

A few days later, I lay in my bed and wept. With genuine trust, I asked God for forgiveness and to take this lump of clay and make and mold me into what He wanted. Almost immediately, I began to panic because I didn't know what to do next. I didn't know how to change. Again His answer came quickly, not in audible words but more of a directive pressing on my heart, "Spend time in the Bible and in prayer and I will transform your life."

I don't remember exactly why I started reading in the Book of Revelation because that is not where I would have chosen to begin seriously reading the Bible. I know without a doubt I was led to read about the Apostle John who was exiled to the island of Patmos for his stand for Christ. During that time, John was given visions and crucial messages that he penned to the churches.

In the third chapter of the Book of Revelation, verses 14 through 21 reads, "And to the angel of the church of the Laodiceans write, These things says the Amen, the Faithful and True witness, the beginning of God's new creation: "I know all the things you do, that you are neither hot nor cold. I could wish you were one or the other! But since you are like lukewarm water, neither hot nor cold, I will spit you out of My mouth! You say, 'I am rich. I have everything I want. I don't need a thing!' And you don't realize you are wretched and miserable and poor and blind and naked. So I advise you to buy from me-gold that has been purified by fire. Then you will be rich. Also buy white garments from me so you will not be shamed by your nakedness, and ointment for your eyes so you will be able to see. I correct and discipline everyone I love. So be diligent and turn from your indifference. Look! I stand at the door and knock. If you hear my voice and open the door, I will come in, and we will share a meal together as friends. Those who are victorious will sit with me on my throne, just as I was victorious and sat with My Father on his throne." (NLT)

When I read these words, I couldn't move. There it was in black and white; exactly what God spoke to my heart in the back of that van. I was lukewarm, neither hot nor cold. There in the quietness of my time with Him alone, it registered that He had been pursuing me all those years. I fully realized His desire for me was a deeper, loyal relationship with Him.

There would be a number of short and powerful heart-to-heart conversations with God in the days to come. These interactions drew me into the practice of a daily quiet time. I made a commitment to set my alarm fifteen minutes early and get up to read the Bible and meet with Him. God has been true to His promise to transform my life through these quiet times. He wants to deepen your relationship with Him and change your life too.

Jesus said, "The thief's purpose is to steal, kill and destroy. My purpose is to give them a rich and satisfying life." John 10:10 (NLT) Christ came to save us and give us full, abundant life in eternity <u>and</u> here on earth. I would venture to say many Christians are not living that rich and satisfying life. I know I wasn't. He's not talking about rich as in money and personal possessions. Jesus is talking about the life He died to give us: unfailing love, peace that goes beyond understanding, an underlying joy even in the midst of problems and pain and the security of being held by a God who will never let go.

Before my eye-opening encounter with God, I was comfortable and complacent in my relationship with Him. Complacency destroys the exciting, purpose-filled life that God wants for us. It kills our effective witness for Christ. I now realize it is a deadly sin that subtly lies. The deception that we can be self-sufficient is one of the most effective lies in Satan's tool bag.

And this subtle sin is rampant among the body of Christ. None of us are immune to it.

I NEVER want to go back to the complacent life I was living, but I am learning how subtly this sin enters into my life. I've been praying for God to reveal any area where I am growing complacent. He is happy to oblige. I've asked Him to alert me when my choices begin to slip into complacency.

I'm now aware of the crux of the problem. I resist Him. Perhaps you are quietly thinking, "I love Jesus. I don't resist Him." That was my first reaction too. Nevertheless I prayed, "Lord, show me where I am resisting you." Turns out, I do it all the time. When I do, my heart grows a little more cool.

I lovingly ask you to use this "list" as a time for self-examination, not condemnation. God is so merciful and compassionate in His discipline toward us. His unfailing love blots out our sins. Here's what He's shown me:

- I resist Him when I refuse to listen and obey the Holy Spirit regarding a sin in my life.
- I resist His gift of forgiveness when I refuse to admit I have committed an offense against Him or others.
- I resist Him when I withhold forgiveness to those who've hurt me.
- I also resist His forgiveness when I have difficulty forgiving myself for past sins and choose shame instead.
- I resist His whisper to simply sit with Him and enjoy Him and the wonder of His creation. I choose busyness.
- I resist His goodness and current provision which shows itself in discontent.
- I resist Him when I don't think I don't need to pray for direction and go my own way.
- I resist His gift of peace and rest when I refuse to come to Him, fall into His arms with my heartaches, problems, hectic schedules and responsibilities. Rather, I choose to be stressed and depressed.
- I resist the Holy Spirit's nudge when I choose Facebook rather than the Good Book.
- I resist his invitation to spend alone time with Him and hit the snooze button.

My list goes on and on. The point is I resist Him. The truth is I don't want to.

Being aware is half of the battle. I want to recognize early on when I am tempted to resist Him and immediately draw near to

Him. I want to be totally and fully submitted to Jesus. I know you do too. I challenge you to make some quiet time and ask the Lord where you may be resisting Him. Allow Him to put your heart in His compassionate hands and insert His spiritual thermometer. Be still and allow Him to talk to you about His diagnosis. The medicine is quiet time. The cure is to love, depend on and obey Him.

Is time spent reading the Bible and praying a priority in your life? Are you excited to see what He will do in and through you each day? Is your love for Jesus growing or growing as tepid as your bathtub filled with hot water neglected too long?

I wish I could come into your home, sit with you and tell you of all the amazing ways He has changed my life. I wish I could explain the peace and security that undergirds my life even in the face of all that is going on around us but of course, I can't. But I can encourage you to allow God to draw you into a deeper, passionate relationship with Jesus by consistently spending time with Him reading the Bible and praying.

The Creator of the Universe wants to spend time alone with you! Let that sink in.

The greatest command given in the Bible is to love God with all our hearts, souls, and minds and to love others. (Matthew 22:37-39) We can't love Him like that if we don't spend regular, quality time to get to know Him better and experience His passionate love nor will we be able to love others.

From the Garden of Eden to Eternity, foremost on God's heart is an intimate relationship with you and me. There can't be intimacy without spending quality time together. Make a commitment to respond to His lavish love. He wants to lead and walk with us through this thing called life. He did not promise it would be easy but He did promise to be our peace through every minute. (John 16:33) Life is hard; He is with us. Time is short; He has stuff for us to do. Life is not perfect but loving a perfect God is life!

Father God, I really want to grow closer to you. I don't want to go through the motions anymore. I don't want to be self-reliant. I want to have a heart aflame for Your Son, Jesus Christ. Help me to make regular time to be alone with You. Help me to see clearly the moment I begin to resist You. I want to live my life allowing You to work in me and through me to accomplish Your perfect will. Please fan the flames of passion for You until the day I draw my last breath. May my devotion to You be so attractive to others, they will desire You too. Help me to recognize and resist the devil and draw near to You. In the sweet name of Jesus, amen.

Chapter Two
Quiet Times

"Come with Me by yourselves to a quiet place and get some rest." Mark 6:31 NIV

Have you ever sat in a elementary school cafeteria and just listened to all the noise? I have, many times and it's not for the faint of heart or the sensitive of hearing. Before he retired, my husband had to wear earplugs at work, OSHA requirement. I don't think OSHA has ever been to a school cafeteria especially a few days before summer break. If they had, teachers would be required to wear earplugs.

We live in a television blaring, radio blasting, horn honking, dog barking, baby crying, kid screaming world with doors slamming, appliances beeping and phones ringing. There are very few places we can go to escape the noise. We look forward to peaceful vacations with visions of quiet rest to kick back and relax... so we pack our iPod, iPad, iPhone, Air Pods, tablet and laptops. Our kids will be sure we don't forget the MP3 player and video games.

Are we afraid to be quiet, still and unplugged or have we become addicted to the noise and busyness?

Have you ever looked out a hotel window onto an interstate, watched the steady traffic rush by and wondered why we're all in such a hurry? We drive at neck-break speeds to cram in as many activities as we possibly can and can't stand to wait 10 seconds for anything only to look at our To-Do lists at the end of the day with a sigh and it's rarely a sigh of satisfaction.

We have become masters at staying busy. From the time the alarm clock blares and our feet hit the floor until we drop into bed each night, our lives are action packed. Reading the Bible and praying are things we try to fit into our busy schedules when we have the time or left-over energy. We tell ourselves we'll make time tomorrow. We lie in bed at night and begin our prayers only to fall asleep long before the "amen".

In our efforts to make life simple and easy, we have complicated our lives and crammed them with so many details of busyness they rob us of valuable time for a deep relationship with Christ and with others. My recent shopping experience drives home this point. I made a cash purchase at a local home improvement store. The cashier rang up the sale and asked me for my address and phone number. Not sure why because I know she wasn't planning on visiting or calling me later. This took several minutes. I gave her my cash. She gave me my receipt as she looked at the next customer.

As I walked to my car, I was transported back in time as a little 9-year-old, pigtailed girl standing in the old country store my Grandfather owned and operated.

"Well hello Russell, how in the world are ya?" My Granddaddy said, as he clutched Mr. Eason's hand and shook it hard.

"I'd be better if we'd just get a little rain. Corn's lookin' mighty poor" he replied as he reached into the cooler for a Coca-Cola. He reached down and popped the top off in the opener on the side of the cooler and removed the glass lid from the jar of crackers. He retrieved a can of sardines from a shelf and pulled back the top. He asked my Granddaddy for the pepper shaker and I've never seen anyone use that much pepper in my little life. They continued their conversation without missing a beat.

"Yep, it sure is dry. I hear that Langston's tobacco has dried up in the field. Shame isn't it? What else can I do for ya today?"

"This'll do, unless you can call down some rain. What do I owe ya?" Mr. Eason said as he finished his snack.

"I'll say a prayer for rain. You can have the sardines but I'm gonna have to charge you for the pepper." My grandfather said tongue in cheek. They both laughed as he took his money and placed it in the cash register. He then turned to walk Mr. Eason to the door.

Even though work was hard and tedious, there was always

time for relationships. When we are faced with choices between a schedule and a relationship, I know what Jesus would choose. I know what my Granddaddy chose. We need to do the same.

It's very easy to dance around the slippery edges of the pitfall of busyness trying to accomplish one more thing until we've slipped into the pit and buried ourselves under a load of work, stress and anxiety. We are guilty of trying to do three things at one time and try to cram yet another activity into our jam-packed schedule. Is this how God meant for us to live our lives? No! Study the life of Christ when He was here on earth.

Right now, you may be screaming for that precious commodity called, time. Maybe your life is in a season that really limits your ability to set aside quiet time. Jesus tells us in the 15th Chapter of John to "Remain in Me, and I will remain in you." He goes on to say in that same chapter, "Apart from Me you can do nothing. But if you stay joined to Me and My Words remain in you..." How do we do that when the minutes in our day seem to be so few?

In leading classes on prayer and speaking to women, I've heard story after story of how difficult it is to find uninterrupted quiet time. Maybe you can relate to Dana's story.

I am going through a season of busyness; one of being pulled in 50 different directions. With all that's going on, my quiet time has really suffered. I am still managing to cling to a few minutes a day, but it's not the same. I mean, I talk to God all day long, but if I'm not taking time to be still and really meditate on His word, it's really just a one-sided conversation isn't it?

My mornings are starting earlier these days and trust me-I am NOT a morning person. (God's still working on that.) I start out with great intentions when I go to bed, but the clock always seems to sound the alarm before my body's ready. I manage to grab a little time in the morning and read a couple of quick devotions, 3-4 verses, jot down a quick line or two and then I'm usually off to the races as the day begins. I'm involved in a precept Bible study that I work on before bedtime, but that's not the same. My journal time has dwindled down to nothing and I know someday I'll regret it. BUT, I also have to remember that God has me right where He wants me. It's my job to pay attention and stop being too busy to listen.

When God grabbed my heart, I began to panic because I didn't know what to do next. I wanted my life to be more than just getting up, going to work, rushing here and there, taking care of my family, falling into bed only to get up and do it all over again. I was ready for my life to be transformed.

When I made that commitment to set aside time to meet with God, read the Bible and to pray, I began to wonder where I was going to fit that into my day. Hmm. I had a major problem...time, or a lack of it I should say. I didn't see how I could cut anything out of my day to exchange it for some time with God. I did come to the conclusion that setting my alarm clock for fifteen minutes before I normally got up wouldn't kill me. I wasn't thrilled about it, but I was relieved to have a plan.

This is the simple note I made about that first quiet time years ago, "I obeyed you, Lord, in Your request that I get up early to spend time with You and read Your Word. I experienced You." Exchange fifteen minutes of sleep to experience the Lord? Let's just say I was more than ready to rise and shine the next morning and it wasn't long until fifteen minutes wasn't enough time.

I want to share when, where and how I usually have my quiet time as an example only. I encourage you to find the method that works for unique you or otherwise you will throw this book in the trash and give up.

When?

Let me start with a caution, do not let anyone tell you when to have your quiet time. We are all different and unique. What works for me may not work for you and vice-versa. We have examples in the Bible of Jesus going away to pray by Himself in the morning (Mark 1:35), in the evening (Matthew 26:36) and sometimes, all night (Luke 6:12) The key to deciding *when* to have your quiet time is answering this question, when are you at

your best? Give Him that part of your day. Don't give Him leftovers when you are tired and exhausted.

Let me suggest that you try to have your quiet time the same time of day so it will become a habit. Are you a morning person? Do you enjoy staying up late? Is the middle of the day when you are at your best? Carve out some time then. You may want to "schedule" this time on your calendar as an appointment that can't be broken unless it's absolutely necessary.

I'm a morning person and a creature of habit so having my quiet time is usually best for me when I first get up. I need this structure to keep this spiritual discipline a habit in my life. By having my quiet time at the same time each day, I can prevent interruptions that might threaten to interfere. If I tried to have my quiet time at night, and I have, I'd be asleep before the first praise song was over, and I was.

I have asked my family not to interrupt me unless someone is bleeding. Just kidding, but if you let those you live with know what you're doing and how important it is to you, hopefully they will respect you and this time. If you have small children, they probably won't understand. Since it wouldn't be very godly to scream, "Can't you see Mommy's having her quiet time!", you'll find encouragement and practical tips from other moms later in this book.

Where?

Find a place alone that is quiet and comfortable. As a nature lover, I'm usually in my favorite chair by a window. Sometimes I choose to have my quiet time on our deck. Other times, when I can wake up enough to change out of my pajamas and put my contacts in, I walk down to the beach with my Bible and journal in hand while the sun is rising. When I go out of town, I have to be really creative to find a spot. I have been known to crawl into an empty bathtub in my pajamas to have my quiet time. A friend uses the closet and a flashlight when she spends weekends away at her family's home. Be creative.

What & How?

The main thing you will need for your quiet time is a Bible. The Bible is the primary means in which God speaks to us. (Read Psalm 19) Your quiet time should definitely center around God's Word. Choose a Bible translation that is Biblically sound and one that you enjoy reading. I choose to use a Bible in print during my quiet time. I guess I'm old-school and I love turning the pages, they sound like angel wings. I write in my bible. I underline and date things. Using a Bible in print makes it easier for me to memorize scripture. But choose what works for you.

You may want to use an on-line Bible. "YouVersion" is my favorite Bible App. It includes devotions, a Verse of the Day, reading plans and of course, the Bible. It also has an audio Bible feature. This is perfect for those who might choose their quiet time on their daily run.

There are many different places you could start if you are new to reading the Bible. I suggest you start in the Book of John. The apostle John was an eyewitness of the ministry of Jesus Christ and this Book gives a beautiful, detailed account of His life. This is where I fell in love with Jesus.

You could read a Psalm each day. You will see example after example of people pouring out their hearts in raw honesty in this collection.

A Proverb a day is another good place to start. There are thirty-one proverbs, one for each day in a month.

You could choose to read through the Bible in one year by using a reading plan. There are many great plans available. Check with your local or on-line Bible bookstore for suggestions. My favorite way to read through the Bible is with a Chronological Bible. I've enjoyed using The Daily Bible in Chronological Order, New International Version published by Harvest House Publishers.

Include praise and worship. You may want to use praise and worship songs in your quiet time. Not because God is an egotistical god, but God dwells in the praises of His people. God

19

delights in our praises and the enemy doesn't. But the enemy has no power over us when we praise. Often, my thoughts are trying to race ahead to my day. Praise and worship helps me to press the "pause" button on my problems, busy schedule, my To-Do list and turns my focus off me and onto Jesus.

You will probably want to use a daily devotional. There are so many great devotionals in print and on-line. Some of my favorite authors are Oswald Chambers, Charles Spurgeon, David Jeremiah, Francis Roberts, Beth Moore and Sarah Young. But there are many, many more. Choose a devotional that is Biblically sound and speaks to your heart.

A word of caution about all things techy. If you use your phone, tablet or computer for Bible reading, devotions or praise music, you may be tempted to check social media, email or texts. If you are trying to break these habits to have your quiet time, use your Bible in print, buy a devotional book and use Alexa set to praise music. Later, when you have developed this discipline and it becomes a regular part of your life, you'll be strong enough to use these technological wonders and resist the temptation.

Gather all these things and place them in your chosen spot now so you won't be searching for them at the beginning of your quiet time. Perhaps you're like me and need a java jolt just to get your eyes open. In the morning, I lumber to the coffee pot then my quiet spot.

Read as much as your heart can take in and time will allow. Some days, I may read several chapters at a time. Then there are days that I plan to read a chapter of scripture only to stop at a single verse that grabs my attention. In the past, I would continue reading because I felt I *had* to complete the Psalm or the chapter. I missed the point... quality not quantity. When a verse or word for that matter, grabs your heart, stop, look and listen. There's a reason it's grabbing your heart. That's where your conversation with Jesus begins.

Sometimes I write the scripture on an index card and tuck it in my pocket or purse before going about my day. I'll bring it out and meditate on it sometimes for many days. I have index cards with scriptures buried like treasures all over my house and car. When I'm searching for something else, I dig one of them up and it speaks to my heart all over again. Other times, I make a screen saver for my phone using a photo and the scripture I'm meditating on. Each time I "open" my phone, I'm reminded to think on it.

Meditate on the scripture. I don't mean sit with your legs crossed and begin some mystical chant. Meditating on scripture is giving God an invitation to search your heart and mind to help you understand, agree with Him and make any necessary adjustments in your thinking and in your life. It's also the opportunity to receive a "jewel" as my friend, Sue calls it when God speaks to her about a specific verse or passage of scripture.

Meditating on scripture is like a cow chewing cud. It will chew on it and swallow it only to bring it up many times to chew on it again. Sorry for that visual but it's important not to rush through this process. We've got to slow down in this fast-paced, instant world we live in. Jesus was never in a hurry and He won't be rushed with us. It's necessary to give the Holy Spirit time to reveal to us what He wants us to see and understand about God's Word.

His Word **teaches** us.

"Make Your face shine upon your servant and teach me your decrees." Psalm 119:135 NIV

His Word **convicts** us of our sins.

"For the word of God is alive and active. Sharper than any double-edged sword, it penetrates even to dividing soul and spirit, joints and marrow; it judges the thoughts and attitudes of the heart. Nothing in all creation is hidden from God's sight. Everything is uncovered and laid bare before the eyes of him to whom we must give account." Hebrews 4:12-13 NIV

His Word **guides** us.
"Your Word is a lamp to my feet and a light for my path."
Psalm 119:105 NIV
His Word **brings joy**.
"Your statutes are my heritage forever; they are the joy of my heart." Psalm 119:112 NIV

From Genesis to Revelation, His Word is His love letter to us. Your love letter to Him is your response to obey. Talk to Him about what you've read or heard in your quiet time. Pray. Talk to Him as you would your best friend, whether you realize it now or not, He is.

The purpose of this spiritual discipline is to take time away from the noise and hurried busyness to still our hearts to be with Him and develop a keen awareness of His presence every minute of our lives. Each day as we enter this quiet time, our hearts learn to take more and more of the still quietness deep into our souls. The peace and quiet becomes more and more a part of us even in the midst of our busy and noisy days. We learn who Jesus is to love Him more and become more like Him when we spend regular time with Him. We gain His perspective on life.

More times than not, something I read in my quiet time comes back at me in the most amazing ways during the day. For example, I had been "perched" on Psalm 91:4 (NIV) "He will cover you with His feathers and under His wings you will find refuge; His faithfulness will be Your shield and rampart." I was preparing a message to deliver at a retreat in Elberta, AL and this verse was the center of the message. That morning my friend Judy, sent me a picture of a dove with her wings spread out to shelter her two baby birds, one under each wing. Although she knows I love birds, she had no idea of the message I was preparing.

Don't just read to check it off your To-Do list, read to know Him more intimately and love Him more and more each day. Look for and make the connections between what you read and the God-moments in your day. Those moments should cause us to stop what we're doing, turn our attention to God and talk to Him throughout the day.

What happens as a result of your quiet time is where the rubber meets the road. We learn more about Jesus to love Him more, become more like Him and live out what we learn each day. This is where the exciting daily opportunities to obey Him, glorify Him and please Him are manifested in our everyday lives. Our everyday raising the family lives. Our everyday going to work lives. Our everyday run errands, shop and carpool lives. Our everyday lives.

Instead of viewing our lives as just going through the motions, we begin to see the exciting and challenging opportunities God places before us. We begin to view life from His perspective. The important things in life are the ones that have eternal value. I have come to learn they are centered around relationships; our relationship with Him and others.

When we rise from our quiet time, we need to "see" that Jesus extends an invitation to us to take His Hand and commune with Him all day long. He asks us to join Him where the Father is working. His Hand is outstretched to you with a smile on His face. Put your hand in His and get ready to really live life.

In Psalm 27:8 (NLT), King David wrote, "My heart has heard you say, "Come and talk with Me." My heart responds, "Lord, I am coming." His highest purpose in life was seeking the presence of God. It should be ours too. There is love, mercy, peace, guidance, forgiveness, joy and fun in His presence.

Spend some time in prayer right now and ask God to show you specifically what He wants you to give up in order to meet with the Lover of your soul. Tell Him you need Him, want Him and really desire to deepen your relationship. Stop! Don't read any further, put your bookmark between these pages and pray now, I'll wait. If you need a prayer starter, here's one...

Lord, I am willing to give up _____ to spend time with You on a daily basis. I ask for You to help me keep this commitment to You. I ask for You to meet me and lead me each day in Your Word and in prayer. I want to know You and love You more. I want to be more like Jesus. Lord, I also confess that I have allowed busyness to creep in and rob me of deep personal relationships with You and others. I confess that I have allowed busyness to rob me of my daily joy in You and others. Forgive me for my sins (name them one by one), cleanse me and prepare my heart for You. I'm excited Lord, keep this excitement for You fresh until the day You take me to heaven. In Jesus' name, amen.

Chapter Three
Listening Is an Act of Love

"My sheep listen to my voice; I know them, and they follow me." John 10:27 NLT

Have you ever met someone who talked nonstop? They talk and talk, ask questions but rarely take time to listen to your answers. Frustrating and annoying, isn't it?

I wonder if God puts His Holy Chin in the palm of His Hand and lets out a long sigh when we talk and talk, ask and ask, but rarely take the time to listen to Him. God invites us to pour out our hearts to Him in our prayers, but good communication involves good listening. We should talk to Him and listen for His voice in our day to day tasks. When we take the time to listen, we **will** hear Him speak.

Do you find it difficult to hear God's voice? Understand, I'm not talking about an audible voice.

But, He is always speaking. Could it be that you simply don't believe He speaks? Maybe you don't recognize His voice because you're busy going your own way. Busy watching TV, texting or addicted to social media. Maybe you have asked but gave up when you didn't hear an answer. We can be such impatient creatures, expecting immediate answers and miss His voice when we plow ahead in our own timing. Perhaps you don't hear Him because you fear Him and imagine Him as a constant critic pointing His finger on your sins instead of the loving and merciful God that He is. He hates sin and uses His lovingkindness to bring us to repentance. He doesn't mind being strong and firm in dealing with our sins but His voice is never condemning. God never torments His children.

One thing is for sure, if we aren't seeking Him, we won't hear Him. When we draw near to Him, He will draw near to us. (James 4:8) If we make it a priority to spend time with Him, He

25

will make sure we hear Him and see Him at work around us.

So how do we calm our anxious hearts, turn down the noise inside our heads and listen? The answer is found in these words "Be still and know that I am God" (Psalm 46:10) We have to simply slow down long enough to get to know Him as Sovereign and recognize that He is our faithful, trustworthy and loving Father. We can trust Him to take care of our every need, our every concern, our every anxious thought. When we take time to recall His faithfulness and goodness, we know He is with us. He will not lead us astray.

During times when I have a major concern, I really struggle to be still. I have to ask Him to remove all the noise in my head and calm my anxious heart. When my troubled thoughts invade the stillness, I stop and talk to God about it. I admit this is the hardest part of communicating with Him. It isn't easy to shut off swirling thoughts of real problems, concerns and pressing to-do lists but I assure you, it is possible. You know why? Because He desires to hear us and speak to us.

There have been many times in my life that it seemed impossible to listen. In those times in my life there has usually been an extreme situation pressing in on me from all sides. When that happens I know I need some serious time alone with God. Time to put my world on hold and be still. I've been to the beach many times alone and there have been many trips to the mountains to a quiet place beside a stream of water. There have been times that I just had a day or an hour at home alone with God. All of these are places I can be still to hear God above the pressing concern.

My first spiritual retreat was an epiphany. I became painfully aware of the noise inside myself and I realized just how easily I was distracted. It wasn't so much that I heard Him speak to me during that retreat as what I left there on the sand. I confessed my busyness and tangled, anxious thoughts. I told Him how difficult it was to give Him full control over my situation and place those I love in His hands.

26

The uninterrupted time was what I needed to honestly express myself and confess my self-reliance and lack of faith. He took my confession, my tangled busyness and anxious thoughts away as I watched a matted cluster of seaweed float out into the ocean. I returned from that trip rested and renewed with a relaxed peace and growing trust. I simply needed His perspective.

A major life event required another spiritual retreat. Just weeks before my son, Steven and my daughter-in-love, Lauren were married, I scheduled a day trip to the beautiful mountains of Valle Crucis, NC. Memory after memory of my son as a little boy reflected against the backdrop of the man he had become and were all swirling in my head. My heart was full of excitement and happiness for him and his bride but reminiscing about his childhood kept my heart at such a tender place, I knew I would be a blubbering mess on his wedding day.

I arrived on a rainy fall day and colorful fall leaves slowly fell to the ground mixed with the raindrops that were falling. On the other side of a little one-lane bridge, I found a spot to pull over and park. A little footpath led to a creek lined with river rock. I took a seat on a large stone purposely set against another to form a bench. There I sat with my umbrella, listening as I watched the water swirl around rocks and hearing the slow pitter patter of a steady shower. My heart showered my eyes with joy-filled tears as I watched each tender memory cross my mind like a tender Hallmark love story. It was beautiful!

I cried and smiled as I recalled his tiny feet taking their first steps, his innocent night time prayers, the sight of his tiny book-bag on his little frame as he graced the doors of his Kindergarten classroom, the day he beamed as he walked across the stage to receive his diploma, and now he was about the walk down the isle with the woman he had chosen to spend the rest of his life with. God and I talked, smiled and laughed for hours about our boy.

I smiled through the entire wedding ceremony.

Most of us are so busy, we feel guilty when we schedule time to do something we perceive as idle. We have become masters at multitasking and feel delinquent when we are still. Many of us are afraid to be alone. These forced times of silence are so desperately needed to break barriers and have a way of driving us into His arms. Being alone can be a spiritual discipline.

The many ways God speaks to us

God has never spoken to me in an audible voice but He speaks to my heart in so many other ways. A few years ago these words jumped off the pages of my Bible in John 15:7, "If you remain in Me and My words remain in you, you may ask for anything you like, and it will be granted!" (NLT) God had been pressing on my heart to call a friend and ask him for a donation to meet a financial need for a ministry I was involved in. Now mind you, I don't go around asking people for money but I felt such an overwhelming necessity to call and ask, I couldn't resist.

I prayed before I called, "God, you know this isn't my style, but I'm trusting you." Then I placed the call and explained the situation and the need. His reply was this, "I will help. One of my life verses is John 15:7..." and he quoted the verse that had jumped off the pages of my Bible earlier that morning. That's just one simple example of how God speaks through His Word!

The Bible is the most important way God speaks to us. His Word is alive and fresh! His Word can cut and heal, comfort and convict, strengthen us and dissolve our insecurities. His fierce love for us flows from every page wooing and pursuing us. His Word is as relevant today as it was when Moses wrote the first five books of the Bible beginning around 1400 BC. When scripture seems to jump off the page at me, He is speaking. When I read a verse in my Bible during my quiet time then later see the same verse in my devotional, He is speaking.

God's Creation displays His glory and majesty daily and I love it when He speaks to me through nature. I remember a time when my husband and I were in our little boat in the Bogue Inlet Bay at Emerald Isle, NC. It was a warm summer day and the sun was playing hide and go seek behind big, puffy, white clouds. The summer breeze made the temperature just right and I was basking in the beauty around me as we drifted by little islands inhabited only by birds. The katydids in the sea grass at the edge of the shore were singing loudly. I suddenly became aware of the symphony of praise being lifted to God from nature and I almost felt like an intruder. The harmony of their song was breathtaking. Perhaps nature sings praises to the Creator every moment of every day we just don't take the time to hear it. What a loss!

When my granddaughter, Carlie, was 1 1/2 years old, we were enjoying an afternoon outside. We sat down beside my flower garden as I picked a bright, orange Zinnia and gave it to her to explore. Just then, the most beautiful black butterfly with gorgeous blue markings flew into the flower garden. Its beauty caught our attention as it softly glided to a flower top. My granddaughter and I were mesmerized. It was as if God spoke these words to my heart with a huge smile on His holy face, "Watch this."

The butterfly gracefully spread her wings in the bright sunshine as if she were on a runway in a Paris fashion show. The sunshine caused colors to emerge that were amazing. It didn't stop there, she seemed to be parading just for my granddaughter as she slowly lifted her wings and turned then closed them again using the flower as her pedestal. My granddaughter pointed to the butterfly. The butterfly did not hesitate but flew directly to the end of her tiny finger. By this time tears were filling my eyes as I exclaimed in my heart, "God, You are amazing!" over and over. The butterfly seemed to kiss the end of her little finger then took flight and floated away. She's sixteen now and that experience was so powerful it seems as if it were yesterday.

The intricate design of all living things is fascinating and God loves it when we pay attention, slow down and listen to Him through nature. He longs for us to simply enjoy (in joy) Him. I notice that when I slow down long enough to enjoy His creation, He speaks.

He can answer a prayer and comfort our hearts through the **lyrics of a song or hymn**. I am so grateful that God inspired King David and others to write the many songs recorded in Psalms. God certainly has used these over and over to speak to me. One of my favorites is Psalm 91. When I am feeling especially discouraged I "dial 911"; Psalm 91:1, "Those who live in the shelter of the Most High will rest in the shadow of the Almighty." God has certainly used Christian music to speak to me, but He also has used all kinds of music to bring comfort or drive a point deep in my heart.

God speaks to us through our **daily experiences**. If I had a choice of cleaning my house or working in my flower garden, I'd be out the door before the duster hit the floor. Don't get me wrong, my house isn't filthy but don't run your finger across the top of the bookshelf. One day I was ashamed when I noticed just how dirty my kitchen floor had become. I chided myself and felt a little guilty for not being more diligent in caring for the inside of my home.

Later that night, I got into bed and read from a little devotional. I could have squealed in delight as I read these words from an entry entitled, "God's Friends" by Joni Eareckson Tada; "...These people had their problems. Nevertheless, Jesus valued them as friends. He didn't expect them to be perfect; He expected them to be themselves, faults and fine points together. And all He asked of them was their love. Love for Him and love for each other. Perhaps you're the type who forgets appointments or birthdays. **Housecleaning doesn't top your priority list. Jesus says that you are His friend if you do two things: love God and love others.**" (Emphasis mine) Had my husband not been asleep, I would have jumped up and down on the bed! God uses our everyday events and circumstances to speak to us. He is intimately personal with every detail of our lives.

In the grocery store, I ran into Becky, a friend and bakery store owner that I had not seen in a long time. We were catching up when a woman holding a can of pie filling politely interrupted, "Is this what you were talking about?" she asked Becky. "Yes", my friend replied. The woman thanked her and returned to her cart.

Becky said, "I just met that woman over by the ice cream. She was looking for something tasty to buy for someone who has cancer. Have you heard about the young mother with tongue cancer? She has a small baby."

"Becky, her name isn't Jamie is it?" I asked holding my breath.

"Yes, it is" she replied.

"That's my nephew's wife", I said with tears beginning to well up in the corners of my eyes.

"Get out!", she said, "She told me Jamie loves blueberries. I told her get a can of blueberry pie filling, come by my shop and I would give her a cheesecake to take to Jamie."

Wow! Coincidence? Absolutely not, they are God-incidents! What an awesome God to orchestrate tiny details to bring joy and revelation of His detailed involvement in our lives and the lives of others even with a simple can of blueberries.

There are so many ways He speaks to us. Are we listening? He longs to speak His lovingkindness over us, comfort and encourage us. Don't just brush these exciting God-incidents away by labeling them as coincidences, you'll miss out on huge blessings.

Prayerfully ask yourself, am I spending quality quiet time with Him to know Him better, love Him more? As we spend time with Him and obey Him we will increasingly recognize His voice. We can't bypass the relationship just to hear answers to our questions and direction for our problems. We are guilty of asking and asking but rarely taking the time to slow down and listen. We are guilty of rushing through each day and fail to enjoy the beauty and awe of nature and ultimately fail to enjoy the Creator.

He really does want to speak His love, truth and peace over us but He won't shout. He pursues us. He waits for us to be still and quiet to listen.

Father God, help me recognize anything that keeps me from hearing You. Help me make the necessary changes in my life to seek You. I need You more than anything. Help me put other things aside and spend time with You. Increase my faith to know that You love me uniquely and desire to be personal with me. In the mighty name of Jesus, amen.

Chapter Four
Write It Down

"We will use these stones to build a memorial. In the future your children will ask you, 'What do these stones mean?'" Joshua 4:6 NLT

There is an awesome miracle recorded in the Third Chapter of Joshua. God led Joshua and the Israelites across the Jordan River into the Promised Land with the priests carrying the Ark of the Covenant. He instructed them to take a few steps into the river and stop. When they did, the flow of water stopped and stayed upstream. The priests stood on dry ground in the middle of the riverbed and the people crossed the Jordan on dry ground. (See Joshua 3:17 NLT)

The story continues in Chapter Four as God instructs Joshua to choose twelve men, one from each of the tribes to take a stone from where the priests were standing, and pile them up where they were to camp that night. Joshua explained to the men that the stones would be used to build a memorial. The memorial would serve as a reminder to them and their descendants of the awesome exodus from Egypt.

The Israelites lived the great miracles we read about in scripture but soon forgot God's faithfulness, instructions, goodness and love. They soon began to grumble and complain. Worse than that, they began to doubt Him. They didn't fully understand what He was doing or where He was taking them...to freedom.

We are no different from the Israelites are we? We experience awesome God moments but let them slip out of our minds and hearts as time passes or when we are faced with the next problem or crisis. We easily forget His faithfulness and goodness which can lead us to doubt. We fail to remember that

He is powerful and mighty, able to accomplish more than we can ask or think. (Ephesians 3:20)

Memorial stones in Biblical times were used to mark the site of a divine revelation or significant event in the life of an individual. (Read Genesis 28:18, 1 Samuel 7:12 for more examples) We all have experienced God's miraculous hand in our lives. We all have those awesome God-moments and personal revelations about God that we need to not only remember but hold tightly in our hearts and minds and sometimes share them.

Keeping a journal is like placing memorial stones. Journaling can help us make the connections in what He says to us and how we respond. Our trust in Him grows stronger when we recall His past faithfulness. Recording scripture, divine revelation or significant events can help us see more clearly the path He is leading us on both in our spiritual and personal lives. It will help us recall every detail so we will give Him praise and trust Him in the present.

God uses my journaling to encourage me in ways that only He can and is a valuable tool in building my faith. It trains my spiritual ears to listen and hear Him when He speaks to me. It helps me recall details that I might otherwise forget. Recording my memorial stones in a journal marked the birthplace of a deeper relationship with Christ.

How Do I Start?

A journal can be anything from an inexpensive wire-bound school notebook to a leather-bound book with blank pages. I like the ones that are about 5 X 7 in size and have lined pages with scripture on each page. These usually run from $7.00 to $15.00. The scripture often speaks directly to my day. I also prefer the wire-bound ones because they stay open easily while I write.

To begin, date the inside cover of your journal making sure to include the year. **Date each entry.** You will be surprised how often you will go back to reread something you wrote months even years ago. The date will be very important when you are searching through years of journaling. You will probably be digging into your pile of journals in the months and years to come to make some very important connections. I sure have!

You may consider using an on-line Journal. One I personally like is an App called "Day One Journal" which is really simple to use and has high reviews. The advantage to a journaling App, is that you can record in it periodically throughout the day as you have thoughts to add since we usually carry our phones with us everywhere. The download is free to use with unlimited entries. Really useful additional features are available with a reasonable membership.

Record what is important to you, in whatever way is best for you but do it immediately. If you don't write it down, you may forget or delay making the connections God wants you to make. You may want to journal:

- Your deepest thoughts and emotions
- Conversations with Him
- Life changing events
- Scripture verses that seem to jump off the pages of your Bible into your heart
- What you believe God is saying and your response
- How you "saw" Him that day through nature, circumstances or another person
- Draw a picture
- Write your heartfelt praises in a song or poem
- Write out your prayers
- Record how His faithfulness and goodness has touched you lately
- Thoughts and concerns over your family and others
- Prayer requests

Pour out the contents of your heart to God in your journal in whatever way is uniquely yours. Anticipate, look for and record the connections to what is said in your quiet time. He will not waste one word.

When something stands out as really special, I "dog-ear" that page (turn the corner down and press a crease) as I write. When you have filled up a journal, write the ending date in the front cover under the beginning date. When it is full, take some time to read (harvest) your journal. Highlighting the important things and list them in bullet form in the front of your new journal.

When you harvest your journal you will be amazed to see the clarity and new growth in your relationship with Him. Your reverence and love for God will grow as you read how He has revealed Himself to you. Your faith will be strengthened and you will stand in awe of Him and the wonderful ways He speaks to you.

Place your "memorial stones" in a journal and soon you will see your relationship with Christ grow deeper and clearer.

Lord, I don't want to miss anything You are doing in my life. I want to agree with You and cooperate with You. Help me record the things You want me to take special note of. I want to remember and proclaim You and all Your awesome ways. In the wonderful name of Jesus, amen.

Chapter Five
Quality Assurance

"Remain in Me, and I will remain in you..." John 15:4 (NLT)

The Holy Spirit raises red flags deep inside to alert us that something is not right as we roll through life pushing aside His call to spend time with Jesus. This is the time to stop and earnestly seek Him for direction. The sooner the better. If we ignore these promptings and plow ahead, emptiness is sure to seep into our hearts.

A few women agreed to share their about their quiet time. We can learn a lot from their experiences. Some of their personal stories broke my heart and at the same time they inspired me. Stories from mothers of small children especially touched my heart and made me want to offer to babysit. Others caring for aging parents or relatives with disabilities that still find time to be with Jesus amazed me. Many responded with their creative ways to carve out space in their day to spend quality time with Jesus. I've included their stories in their own words in hopes that you can relate to at least one of them and know you are not alone. I pray they touch your heart, encourage and motivate you.

Brooke

This young woman feels guilty because she is so exhausted and I guarantee she's not alone. Can't you just see the endless responsibilities and guilt of new mommy, Brooke, in her short reply?

It's probably all she had time for!

I have time at the end of the day when the kids are bathed and in bed...lunch packed, (teaching) plans done... I feel guilty because I am so exhausted....I can't tell you how many times I talk to God and don't even get to the Amen .... Zzzzzzzz!

Merriam-Webster's describe guilt like this; "a: the state of one who has committed an offense especially consciously", and **"b: feelings of deserving blame especially for imagined offenses or from a sense of inadequacy"** (Merriam-Webster.com)

We can be guilty of wasting time, of course, but unwarranted guilt alone is a pitfall and hinders us in our relationship with Jesus. Don't mistake inaccurate guilty feelings as conviction of a sin. You may be shouldering mistaken guilt because you had to put down your Bible to pick up your waking baby. Being a mother is a huge responsibility but it's also a privilege and high priority that God has given you.

I won't throw an "It's OK, don't worry about it" blanket on everyone who is feeling guilt because maybe you have substituted this very important part of your relationship with Jesus by choosing social media, texting, work, shopping, TV, books or magazines instead.

Social networking has especially captivated the attention of many women and drained the time right out of their clock. As my friend, Beth Ann says, "Facebook has replaced His Good Book". I can't excuse you, that's something you need to take up with Jesus. If you don't currently have a quiet time, pray and ask Him to reveal any activity that is wasting your time. Ask Him to help you cut it out of your day to make time for Him.

If social networking has a ball and chain around your life, put down the phone, turn off the computer. Delete the tweet, roast the post and nix the text. Delay the Instagram, nip the Snapchat, forfeit the on-line game and Knick knock the Tik Tok. Why? Because the Creator of the Universe longs to spend time with you, **quality time.**

Dawn (raising 3 children)

Dawn's story relates how God convicted her and recaptured her wandering heart.

38

At first I thought I was going to take a nap, but God had other plans for my serious quiet time that didn't involve sleep, or blogging, or making a phone call. He got my attention and we had a heart to heart. Wow. The power of getting quiet and being still in front of the Lord is amazing. I had my Bible, my journal, and my iPod. I listened to two songs that have been really speaking to me. I was able to really talk and listen to God and He revealed so many things to me in this hour that we had together. I realized a list of things that I needed to let go of, to set free and put into His hands. I didn't want to carry the burden of these things any longer and He didn't want me to. He also brought it to my attention that I have been asking Him for direction and answers and I haven't been available to listen to what He has been telling me. I thought He was silent, because that does happen, but He wasn't. I just wasn't listening.

My serious quiet time is something I realized I have been missing over the last few months. This experience is a necessity that I forgot about, and that can't happen any longer. He is the strength and the answer to what I need to live a life full of joy. So often I overlook having a quiet time. I pray a lot during the day, but a serious quiet time—where I can reflect and listen—I put aside. I become too busy to stop, be still and be amazed by Him, and when I forget, I am lost. My days don't go right, I get nothing done and all along I had the answer right in front of me—look to Him! He has the answers, the directions, the strength, the comfort, the companionship and the love I need.

He stands ready to grab your drifting heart too and pull it close to him.

Alysia

Alysia's story reminds us of how much we need God through the busy season of motherhood and encourages us to put Him first.

When I reflect over the past 15 years, I see how God has drawn me closely to his side through a season that could be described as busy, overwhelming, and just plain crazy!!!

When my youngest daughter was very small, a well-meaning more mature woman encouraged a group of us "young-uns" not to be too concerned about finding time for our relationship with the Lord. She said that the demands of being a wife and mother are so great that the most any young mother could hope for was a quick prayer or a one-minute devotional each day. While I expect she wanted to relieve us of the stress of "one more thing," following her advice would have resulted in a downward spiral for me spiritually and emotionally.

As children came and responsibilities increased, I discovered that I had never needed God more! My busy season of life drove me to his feet, where I found true direction, encouragement, and guidance. While the world around me seemed to be defining me by the success of my baby's naps or the way he behaved in the church nursery, I was beginning to find my significance and value in my Heavenly Father's love. I began to discover that there was more to life than just what I could see; I started to understand that God was weaving a beautiful tapestry over time and that he was calling me to be part of HIS story!

Looking back on those years, God opened doors for me to be involved in women's Bible studies and my relationship with Him flourished. I found that the accountability of being part of a group study was the encouragement that I needed to follow hard after God even during a busy, stressful season. Now that my kids are 14, 12, and 9, the "deposits" that God allowed me to make in my relationship with Him during those "young-un" years are priceless.

As a friend once told me, we all tend to suffer from "once-itis." You know...once I get married, I'll take my walk with God seriously...once I have kids...once I get them out of diapers...once I get them into school...and it goes on and on. I would encourage young mothers to guard their time with the Lord and to find time to build relationships with godly friends. For the past 10 years I've been part of a group of Christian girlfriends who have met to laugh, pray, and hold each other accountable. *As life goes on, I've found that it can get more complicated rather than less (sorry for that news!), but those friendships that started when our children were young have become strong blocks in the walls of faith that God has constructed.*

Motherhood (at any season) can leave a woman exhausted, overwhelmed, discouraged, and isolated, but that is not God's design. Through the chaos, He makes His presence known in our lives, and that is a gift that we cannot afford to miss!

Denise C.

Denise gives us a glimpse into her busy days as she has a small child to raise and offers creative tips to find quiet time.

I make quiet time by using the very first part of nap time as my "sit down and open my Bible" time when I possibly can. If I don't do it first thing during that quiet house time, I am less likely to do it because I see so many things I can get done!! I am working on my prayer life because it seems to always be sporadic. But I'm trying.

I feel very guilty when I don't have a quiet time. One summer, I think my daughter was right at 2 years old, I lost it. I just felt like I was in a confused daze and had no idea what direction my life, spiritual or otherwise, was going. I was more emotional and not a great support to my husband although I was pouring myself into the care of our little girl. That's when I decided to go to Bible study that Wednesday night and God told me through the lesson and what was spoken and studied... "Come back to your Bible and pray to Me and I will put you back on track."

I did and He did.

Others are slaves to quiet time comparisons. They measure the quality of their quiet time to the minute hand on the clock. If someone mentions their long quiet time, they feel they don't measure up and the result is guilt. We feel so guilty about not spending an hour in our quiet time that we can't love the relationship with Jesus that we do have. Jesus doesn't have His stopwatch out to see how you measure up. I'm pretty sure He doesn't have one. He longs to hold you close to His chest and talk with you. He knows every detail of your hectic schedule, every day. He knows your family obligations and your work schedule. He is not checking your quiet time performance with a checklist. He extends grace and love but He desires intimacy which is found in quality time with Him.

Tami

Tami is a Women's Ministry Director and shares her wise heart.

When you don't have (invest) as much time as you think you should, guilt creeps in and it is typically masterminded by the enemy. Guilt turns into condemnation and more time is spent fretting over not having a QT than it would take to actually have a productive and meaningful time with the Lord. Also, it seems like many judge others and think they should have a cookie-cutter quiet time. I believe quiet time's to be as unique as we are.

If you're a mom with small kids, you're lucky to go to the bathroom for some peace and quiet and even then the kids are knocking on the door, saying "Mommy, Mommy" over and over. When that doesn't work, they start sticking their little fingers under the door. Your quiet time could consist of using a promise box. You can make your own with index cards and write scripture verses on them or store-bought ones at your local Bible bookstore or on-line. Read and meditate on one scripture. Put it on the refrigerator door or in your pocket. Think and talk to Him about it throughout the day. You may choose to use a 5-minute devotional. The point is to stay connected with Jesus, abide in Him. Turn your attention to Him throughout the day. Retreat to the inner sanctuary in your heart for some quiet time, no matter what you're doing. Talk to Jesus throughout the day and exclaiming, "Oh, Lord!" when they color on the walls doesn't count.

Lauren

My Daughter-in-Love, Lauren has a life and schedule this year that is stretched to say the least.

Quiet time is something that is hard to find in the life of a mother with small children. The pleasure of being a mother is the greatest thing in the world. However, this year has been the busiest in my life. I'm a mother with a full-time job and going to school for my Master's Degree to obtain my Neonatal Nurse Practitioners license. This has required me to work additional 12 hour shifts for clinical in addition to my regular 12-hour shifts. We also welcomed our most exciting and wonderful surprise at the beginning of 2020, our third son to complete our family of five.

Having two wild and rambunctious boys and a baby that is proving to follow in their footsteps on top of my other responsibilities, has made it stressful and really hard to find quiet time. I pray daily, mainly right before going to bed. I pray for the health of my family and the strength for me to get through this time in my life, and I pray for the Lord to help those who need it the most. I know the Lord has a plan for me and testing the amount of strength and stress I can endure has definitely been part of His plan this year. Having said that, I am grateful.

I also love going for walks before taking a test to help clear my head while listening to Lauren Daigle. I had forgotten how much it helped and have been skipping that portion of my testing days until recently and it really paid off.

Being a new mother, I also am still pumping to provide milk for my little giant and those times are the perfect time, especially at work, to sit back and take deep breaths and try to relax and regroup.

Quiet time is needed in everyone's life it's just how you try to get it squeezed into your schedule, even the times driving down the road listening to K-Love or Lauren Daigle counts. Every little minute one can get in, makes a huge difference in the outlook and adds to a healthier mind set in life. If I can do it during this crazy time in my life, I know others can too.

43

Susan

Susan's devotion to God through her devastation is so evident through her words. I don't personally know this precious woman and I don't know if her circumstances drove her into the arms of Jesus. We all have the same twenty-four hours in a day as Susan. Even through all her responsibilities and concerns, she's made her relationship with Jesus high priority. I want to be wholeheartedly devoted to Jesus before devastating circumstances occur, don't you?

My name is Susan I have three young children and my husband was diagnosed almost three years ago with a progressive terminal illness.

Prayer time is essential to our family and myself. I spend 20 to 30 minutes every morning in devotion and prayer. Before my kids leave for school or on the way to school, we have group prayer time. We pray that their daddy's disease stops and for each other and for the day's activities. We all also have prayer at night. A lot of times after the kids are in bed and I lay down and just talk to God about everything.

I had a preacher tell me once that you should be able to talk to God like you talk to a best friend and so that is what I do at night. I would not be able to make it through each day knowing that I'm going to lose my husband before I'm ready for it; without my faith, my prayer or my God. I do have to say that we trust God to take care of us for everything!

Pat

Pat's story reflects her devotion and determination to stay connected to Jesus through circumstances of caring for aging parents and a sister-in-law with a mental disability.

I absolutely have to make time to spend with God or I'm sunk! Yes, I'm very busy with work, family, and church – but I couldn't make it without Him. 14 years ago in March my Mom had an aneurysm that ruptured (on Easter morning at church).

Long story short, she was in the hospital for 110 days – she really shouldn't have lived. Since that time, she's had a feeding tube, can't stand, can't do anything for herself for almost everything and requires 24 x 7 x 365 care. My Dad (bless his heart – every woman should have a husband like him) is her primary caregiver. I live approximately 4 miles away. After I get off work I go to their house (along with my great husband) to do dinner, etc.

Almost 3 years ago we sold our home and built on to and moved with my in-laws to care for them due to their health and also because I have a "mentally challenged" Sister-in-law that we would someday be responsible for. My husband did most of the care for them – but I was "in charge" of the house and a lot of their needs when necessary. We lost both of them this past year and now we have my 59-year-old Sis-law to care for.

I feel it's been a privilege and a gift from God that all this has happened – there has been so many blessings. But I couldn't have made it without Him – he gives me guidance and peace each step of the day.

I have to have time with Him –just like I have to have time with my earthly husband. I get up earlier than everyone else for MY time with God – even if it's only 15 minutes. Sometimes it's even while I'm eating a bowl of cereal if I happen to have a really hectic morning (yeah – I have "milk splashes" on my some of my Bible pages as reminders). Yes, a lot of time I feel guilty about not having enough time – but I try to continue in my car as I go here and there.

Sonja

    Yes, I do have a regular quiet time. I would be in big trouble if I didn't and Jesus is the only one who wants to talk to me early in the morning. I usually read a devotional, my Bible and then pray. I do my Bible study at a different time. If I didn't have my quiet time I wouldn't be prepared for what would come my way that day. To those who have not yet developed this spiritual discipline, I urge you to do it! Do it now because you must learn to discern God's voice from all the other voices. I feel we are in a time of seeing God separate the Wheat and the Tares. (Read Matthew 13:24-30)

Brenda

    This is from Brenda who is co-raising her grandchildren with her single daughter.

    This season I'm in is not the season that "should" be for me right now, but Daddy has me here. I'm in what they say is pre-retirement years at age 58. I have worked 43 years, mostly full time, raised children and two stepchildren in former marriage. My daughter, and I are jointly raising two more little ones which are my grandchildren. This came about from a tragic abusive situation. Moving through these troubled waters and seeing how faithful God is has been a moving experience yet, I've still had times that all I could do was pray. I work from 7-4, pick up the grandkids, make dinner, homework, get ready for bed, and wait until my daughter arrives home from a first responders career each night. Drive home at 10 or 11. Start over again the next day.

    With that all said, Do I have a specified quiet time? Well, I have quiet time at different times, sometimes a couple times a day. I read Scripture and pray. I pray while I fold their laundry and ask God for the ability to do everything while fighting selfish resentment. I ask for help to focus on the blessings of being with my grandchildren. I pray for patience to deal with these beautiful high energy children! I feel so blessed to share Jesus with my grandchildren. Sometimes I say to the Lord, "I'm too tired, in too much pain, this is not fair. Then those emotions melt away as I feel the Lord giving me the ability to meet the challenges. I can then listen to Him quietly calling me each day to be still and just focus on Him. My quiet time consist of reading my Bible or I just pray in silence not saying much, just being in His presence.

For the grandmothers who may find themselves in a season like this...well it seems the same season as being a young mom. The difference is your bones may crack more and you may move slower. When I was younger and raising small children, I had to learn that quiet time doesn't have to be set in stone. I learned that to spend time with the LORD could be at anytime and anywhere! Giving Him first place in my life is what is important. In these latter years of my busy life, I don't let guilt of not having a "perfect quite time" be another hindrance of just spending quiet time with the Lord.

Sue

Sue has maintained a quiet time for many years, she offers her perspective and encouragement.

How do you grow close to someone without talking and acknowledging Him in your everyday walk of life? Develop a time set apart with God the Father, Jesus our Savior, and our personal helper, the Holy Spirit. I know all three are one, but it helps me at times to recognize and call on each One separately.

Each moment you spend with Him will help you grow close. The closer you become, your love grows stronger just as with anyone else you come to love.

During your quiet time, please read His Word, asking the Holy Spirit for wisdom and understanding. That's how you will hear Him talk to you. The more you are able to spend time, the more you will learn to recognize your spirit receiving His Word. Through the years, you will walk closer and closer with Him. It is a joy the world can never offer.

Jill

My other Daughter-in-Love, Jill offers her thoughts on her evolving quiet time and how she combats the serious challenges of Covid-19.

As a mom of two always-on-the-go boys, finding time to be still has not been by chance. My quiet time has changed over the years. When they were babies, quiet time was when they were asleep in my arms. When they became toddlers and preschoolers, quiet time was at night after they were in bed asleep. As they've gotten older and are now preteen/teen, it can be early. In the morning before everyone is awake, in the evening on a jog, during a lunch break or even when I'm opening up my laptop waiting for programs to load. Sometimes quiet time is reading the Bible, praying or writing in my prayer journal. Even praising and singing Lauren Daigle or King and Country (loudly and off-key) while cleaning the bathroom can be quiet time and worship for me.

The one commonality between them all is gratitude. The gratitude that I experience for God and express to God.

Sometimes life interrupts quiet time and it ends sooner than hoped or planned. There is always noise all around including the commotion that Covid-19 has caused. (I am now working from home and overseeing my two middle schooler's on-line school work.) But, when I can let go of the chaos and noise as God commands in Psalm 46:10, He says, "Be still, and know that I am God." By saying a simple thank you to God, He fills my heart with peace. The more thanks given, the more moments He fills.

I think it's cool that after the psalmist quotes God's command to be still, in the following chapter he says to shout and sing and clap hands and sound trumpets in giving praise. When I give thanks and praise, I am able to let go of the noise and chaos and experience more quiet and more stillness.

If your family responsibilities have you pressed for time to read the Bible, pray and journal, remember this is a season in your life and it will pass. However, don't let your circumstances give you an excuse not to spend time with Jesus. Go to Him first with quality time and you will find that your schedule will be more productive. Don't believe the lie that you are too busy. Don't give in to the temptation to give up, telling yourself you will find time when your circumstances change. Purposely step around that pitfall of guilt. Don't beat yourself up over time you don't have, focus on quality. Stop fretting, be creative and be joyful when you make treasured time.

Father God, You see my life, my responsibilities and my activities. I bow down and lay it all at Your feet. I ask that You take away all invalid feelings of guilt and replace them with peace and contentment in this season of my life. I ask that You convict me of time I am wasting that I could be spending with You. I ask that You help me see specifically where I can make the most of my days to Your glory, my good and for the benefit of everyone I come in contact with. Help me listen as You direct me and help me obey. I need You and desire to spend time with You in the midst of my busy days. In the mighty name of Jesus, amen.

Chapter Six
I'm Here, God, But My Thoughts Aren't

Psalms 103:14 "For He knows how weak we are; He remembers we are only dust." (NLT)

Quiet time is exasperating when your head is full of noise. It is very difficult to be still and quiet when your mind is shouting your list of problems and concerns or your to-do list one item at a time, isn't it? Have you ever read a portion of scripture with your eyes but your mind has long checked out? Me too. I am frequently plagued with the inability to just focus. My mind is foggy and I just have trouble keeping my wandering thoughts corralled.

Take a peek into my mind for an example (warning, it's a scary place). I begin reading at Matthew 6:25, "So I tell you, don't worry about everyday life - whether you have enough food, drink, and clothes. Doesn't life consist of more than food and clothing? Look at the birds. They don't ..." *Birds. I need to fill the bird feeders. I don't have much bird seed left, need to make a stop by Tractor Supply. Oh I need to go by the grocery store too. I can pick up some milk while I'm there and check to see if there is something I can fix for dinner this weekend. Wonder if it will be warm, I really need to work in my flower beds and get some weeding done.* My mind connects in the middle of verse 30, "...wonderfully for flowers that are here today and gone tomorrow, won't He more surely care for you? You have so little faith!"

Then I realize my eyes have read several verses of scripture, but I don't have a clue what I read. This reminds me of a more dangerous situation in an early morning drive to work. I'm sure you can relate. Have you ever wondered if you stopped for a traffic light long after you realized you went through it? Can you believe we're all on the highway together?

What do we do when our wandering thoughts and busy schedules take our minds on a run we never intended to take? Early on, I tried to cover up these thoughts and pretend they weren't happening. If I was honest about the detour my mind just took on the path of wandering thoughts, I might have to admit that scripture just wasn't holding my attention. If I was honest about my to-do list shouting louder than the Words of Christ, I might have to surmise that I believe my list is more important.

So here it is, a big boulder in my path to quiet time and I'm going to pretend it's not there. That didn't work for me. Probably won't work for you either. Here's why, God requires honesty. Honesty in everything. I'm learning to turn to Jesus quickly and confess. I explain what is happening even though He already knows and say, "Lord, please help me stay focused."

I love Psalm 139, God knows our thoughts and knows everything about us. It is silly to try to hide anything from Him. This Psalm helps us know that He loves us despite all our wandering ways. Psalm 103:14 says He knows we are but dust.

A friend is facing some very serious health issues. When she comes into her quiet time, is she just supposed to push back those looming thoughts? Should she try to hide the fact that the chemotherapy has made her mind like mush and her thoughts run together like water? No! Her quiet time is the place to run to Him and tell Him all that is on her heart and mind to receive His comfort, strength, and love. He is her safe place to unload and unpack. He's our safe place too.

Wandering thoughts rob us of precious time, so we need to be quick to recognize when our thoughts have set out on their own. We need to do all we can to corral and focus our thoughts so we can have quality time with Jesus. Quality time to praise Him, learn from Him, worship Him, talk to Him, listen to Him, and love Him more.

I pray these strategies I use to help me regain focus will help you too.

Admit your inability to focus. Talk to Him honestly about whatever is stealing your thoughts and ask for His help. Give God your desire to maintain quality quiet time and ask Him to help you. He will. Rest in the assurance and truth that He desires your company. He would move heaven and earth to be with you and me. He did that when He sent Jesus to die for us on a cross. Rely on the truth that He loves you fiercely. He sees into your heart. He understands and is willing to help.

Keep a notepad or sticky notes in your quiet time spot. When sudden thoughts infiltrate your mind, such as; *I need to call the water company, I need to pick up bread,* write them down. Get them off your mind and onto paper so you can deal with them after your quiet time. I used to be so worried about forgetting the reminders that I wasn't fully engaged. As long as you aren't spending your quiet time making out your daily to-do list, it is helpful to write your reminder down and then move on.

Sometimes we have serious problems that are looming in front of our minds like mountains and we just can't seem to concentrate on anything else. He understands that. He wants you to come to Him with all your fears and emotions and talk to Him about them. He is the safest place to keep your emotions in check and to hold your deepest thoughts. But sometimes we seem to repeat our problems day after day. If you determine that your thoughts are invaded by worries and concerns, stop and make a list in your journal. Offer the list to your Heavenly Father. Thank Him for knowing all your needs and rest in His tender care for you. Find scriptures that speak to that concern or scriptures that comfort you and write them on notecards. Put the notecard in your pocket or purse and carry it with you all day, taking it out often to read it and pray using that Truth.

Don't fall into the pit of despair by continually telling God how big your problems are. Declare your trust in God by telling your problems how big your God is.

Read scripture out loud. This helps me tremendously when my thoughts are wandering and I am having trouble focusing.

There's something about seeing scripture in print, speaking and hearing it that helps me regain sharp focus.

But maybe you repeatedly have trouble staying focused as you read. Perhaps your Bible translation is difficult or not the best for you to read and enjoy. Ask your Pastor or a godly friend to suggest a different Bible translation for you. However, be sure it is a translation that is accurate.

Maybe you need structure in reading the Bible. Find and use a Bible reading plan. Check with an online Bible Bookstore or Google "Bible Reading Plans". Choose one, print it out and keep it with your Bible.

Another pitfall we need to be mindful of is we are all subject to turning a good discipline into a dead ritual. He knows if you are just "putting in time" to check "Quiet Time" off your to-do list. If this is the case, confess it. If you don't, you may find yourself eventually in the rut of a meaningless quiet time. Don't try to cover that up - won't do any good. Confess it and ask for His help in making your time together vibrant and beautiful. Be encouraged that He sees your desire. Ask Him to deepen your desire to spend quality time with Him to know Him better and love Him more. Try changing your quiet time a bit. Try going for a walk when you normally curl up in a chair.

I have also found that there is a direct correlation to my wandering thoughts and my busyness. Take some time to honestly evaluate your activities. Make a list of how you spend your time on a daily basis for one week. Spend some time prayerfully considering the importance of each activity. Determine where busyness has overtaken the necessary. Discover where busyness has taken priority over important relationships, especially your relationship with Jesus. Confess it and agree with Him over it. Ask Him to help you make the necessary changes in your schedule to make lifelong positive adjustments.

Write these down in your journal and review them often. Give yourself regular checkups. Celebrate your progress and determine in your heart to press on. Ask God to order your day and your list of things to do. Ask Him if there is anything you can eliminate. He is the keeper of all time. He knows what is important. He knows what "interruptions" are necessary in our day as well. Those usually turn out to be "opportunities".

Getting rid of the noise inside your head and maintaining focus requires commitment and discipline but with God's help, it can become easier.

Lord, You made me. You know everything about me. Forgive me when I try to hide my thoughts from You. Lord, I'm struggling with wandering thoughts. Take them captive and obedient to You. Lord, I'm giving You permission to search my mind and heart to determine where I need to make permanent changes in my activities to spend quality time with You. Lord, increase my desire to love You and others. In the powerful name of Jesus, amen.

Chapter Seven
I'm Here God. Are You?

"The Lord Himself goes before you and will be with you; He will never leave you nor forsake you. Do not be afraid; do not be discouraged." Deuteronomy 31:8 (NIV)

We all go through seasons of feeling distant from God. I can't tell you why you may be feeling this way. Only God can bring you to the reason and remedy. I will tell you that the many times I have experienced this feeling, there have been just as many reasons: unconfessed sin, busyness, failure to receive His deep love and God stretching my faith, are just a few.

During these times when I am feeling distant from God and searching for the reason, I often feel as though I am just going through the motions in my quiet time. It seems lifeless and I feel as though I am just checking off, "Quiet Time", on my to-do list.

I want to deeply enjoy God and my relationship with Him every minute. I want to delight myself in Him every day. These times of feeling distant threaten my quiet time. Day after day of feeling as though my prayers are hitting the ceiling cause me to consider giving up the time I've set aside to meet Him when it seems He isn't here. Do you ever feel this way?

The truth is, He IS here even when we don't "feel" Him with us. His Word promises us that He will never leave us or forsake us. We have to cling tightly to that promise during these times and look expectantly for Him to reveal what He wants us to recognize and understand.

These times can cause us to give up our daily appointment with God, which is exactly what the enemy hopes we'll do. Or they can cause us to really press into Him. That's exactly what God wants us to do.

When my kids were little and became extremely panicked

55

about something, they would jump at my feet screaming and yelling. It was hard to get them to be quiet enough for me to talk to them to calm and reassure them. I would often squat down and get eye to eye with them, put their little chin in the palm of my hand and say nothing. When I had their undivided attention, I could quietly soothe their fears.

I think sometimes God has to do that with us. He watches over us while we refuse to seek or listen to His Truth. When we get to the point that we feel as if we're talking into the wind, He stoops, holds our chins in His Palm of His Holy Hand and says nothing until He has our undivided attention, then He speaks Truth into our hearts.

Ill share an example that really stands out in my mind. He held my chin in the cup of His Hand in such a beautiful way.

I was tired and worn out from trying to "cross my t's and dot my i's" to remedy the distance I felt from God. I kept thinking that if I could only "do" my quiet time "correctly" I would sense His presence again. I thought, "Surely, I must be doing something wrong". Later, one morning while vacationing at the beach with my friend Sonja, I rose early for my quiet time. I decided I'd had enough. I was so tired of agonizing over what I was doing wrong. I wasn't going to spend another morning trying to make my quiet time "perfect" I opted for a walk by the sea instead of my usual, routine quiet time ritual that I had fallen into.

The beach was almost deserted as I breathed deeply the beauty of the sky and sea. The sun was still hiding behind the dark blue water as it threw incredible colors of orange, red and purple across the sky. The wind playfully tossed my hair back and forth as the sea mist introduced me to the morning and chased the sleep from my head. The gentle roll of the sea as it fell to the surf filled me with peaceful awe and the sudden awareness of His Presence walking with me. The absolute beauty of the morning and His presence took my breath away. There were no words as we walked. I was exhilarated and content all at the same time, enjoying His awesome presence and quietly resting in it. "Now this is what my quiet time should be like" I thought, as a shell caught my eye.

I walked to the lone white shell lying on the wet sand and reached to pick it up. Disappointed, I saw that it had a small hole through it. I identified it as an Angel Wing Shell. These beautiful shells do not often grace the beaches. They are about four inches long and look just like what you would imagine an angel's wing to look like. They are very fragile and thin.

Because it was broken, I decided I didn't want to keep it. I mean who wants a broken shell, right? I tried to toss it back onto the sand, but I was captivated by it. I took another look at it. It was then that I heard His undeniable voice as He spoke to my heart. I "heard" Him say, You are My angel. You look for perfection to satisfy Me, but I love you the way you are, imperfections, weaknesses and all. My thoughts are not your thoughts; My ways are not your ways. You see yourself as imperfect trying to earn my love. I see you through the blood and body of My Son who has made you whole.

I worshipped Him that moment, I mean I really worshipped Him. I worshipped Him without all my little legalistic rituals. I experienced how wide, how long, how high and how deep the love of Christ is for me and I was filled with all the fullness of God. I kept that broken Angel Wing Shell until it finally disintegrated into pieces. All the other perfect shells in my collection couldn't compare to that one. It remains my all time favorite. The memory still reminds me of how much He loves me, imperfections, weaknesses and all. It reminds me of the love of Christ that makes me whole. I don't have to be perfect, just devoted.

Sometimes these seasons of feeling distant from God seem as if they will never end. But if we press into God instead of giving up and drifting away, the result can be a deeper and stronger relationship with Christ. There is always something to learn.

When you experience these feelings of being distant from

God. Don't try to pretend they aren't real. Stop and pray. Ask God to give you wisdom and lead you to His truth. Consider asking your spouse or a close friend to pray for you.

God gave us feelings and emotions to enhance our lives not control them. Always, always hang your hope in the Truths of His Word, not your fickle feelings. Search the Bible for scriptures that describe His faithfulness. Write them in your journal. Write them on your phone. Write these scriptures on index cards to tuck in your pocket, purse, and car. Slap them up on your mirror and the front of the fridge. Tape them to your forehead, for crying out loud. Keep them tucked deep in your heart to remind you that He **is** near.

I'll give you the first one, and don't you ever forget it...

"The Lord Himself goes before you and will be with you; He will never leave you nor forsake you. Do not be afraid; do not be discouraged." Deuteronomy 31:8 (NIV)

Did you write it down? Go on, do it.

While we make the habit of quiet time each day, we run the risk of the repetitive appointment becoming routine and mundane. I am a creature of habit but I also have to fight boredom in my life. I'm the kind of girl that likes to move furniture around, hang my pictures in different places. If I'm not careful, my routines and daily schedules can become stale and monotonous. When I am feeling as if my quiet time is falling into a rut, I know I need to make some changes.

Moving from my corner of the living room to the porch or to another room can breathe fresh air into my quiet time. I may grab my phone and earbuds and listen to praise and worship music as I take a walk before sitting to read my Bible. Change the environment and scenery to paint fresh colors on the walls of your quiet time.

Press in and press on. Don't give up and don't give in to the thoughts of abandoning your special time with God. Don't drift into a sea of mediocre commitment that He is repulsed with. Give it all you've got. Keep praying and seeking Him until He brings you to the Truth and cure of feeling distant from Him.

Father God, help me as I struggle with the feeling of wondering where You are right now. Forgive me for accusing You of abandoning me. Give me strong faith to hold on tight to Your promise that You are always with me. Give me understanding and wisdom. Revive and refresh my time with You each day. Bless me with a keen awareness of Your presence in my quiet time and my day. In the mighty name of Jesus, amen.

Chapter Eight
Who's the Focus?

"Let the godly sing with joy to the Lord, for it is fitting to praise Him". Psalm 33:1 NLT

My husband and I have a little boat we love to take out into the Bogue Inlet Bay around Swansboro, NC. There are many beautiful deserted little sandy islands just waiting to be explored. We also enjoy throwing a hook or two into the emerald-blue water. The sea is usually clear and calm, however when the wind kicks up and the tide flows, the calm water can grow choppy. When fishing in rolling swells, you'd better keep your eyes on something in the distance. To focus on the edge of the boat and each surge in the water is asking for a wave of nausea or worse.

When we focus on our circumstances, problems and concerns, they tower before us making it difficult to see the big picture. We become so focused on our difficult situation that we lose our view of God. We focus on the immediate and allow the truth of God to fade into the background. Doubt and fear seep into our hearts and minds and drown our faith. Praise and encouraging words are replaced with grumbling and complaining.

Who is your focus during your quiet time? I have to ask myself that question on a regular basis. My devotion is in Jesus Christ but my eyes turn to me, me, me more often than I care to admit. My focus slowly shifts from the magnificence of Jesus, His love, joy, power and ability; to the cruel, sad, perverse state of the world and its effects on myself and those I know and love.

Sometimes I'm just downright selfish. My quiet time becomes one sided as I ask and ask focusing on my needs, my wants, and my desires until I need a serious adjustment in my spiritual focus.

However, I've heard story after story from women facing serious problems with major concerns and my heart aches for them. These are just a few examples of real people with overwhelming situations. There's Karen, who battles insecurity of epic proportions after being mentally and physically abused at the hand of her mother. Sharon thought she had a happy marriage until her husband of 27 years blindsided her with a request for a divorce. Sonia's daughter is killing herself with an eating disorder.

Closer to home, my 7-year-old grandson became septic after an infection in his little hip and fought for his life while the doctors tried to find the right combination of antibiotics. There's my young nephew who lost his wife to cancer at age 26. They'd only been married a few years with a baby boy. My neighbor lost his job after years of loyal service. He's 55 years old.

I know you could give me story after story too. You may be living some of these examples yourself. Day after day of facing what seems like a dead-end situation can consume our every thought.

But here's a Truth you can hang every problem, trouble and concern on; God is with you. He will never leave you or forsake you. He has never taken His eye off of you, not for one second. He desires your company and He is the one to run to when life crashes around you. He is your safe place to run and fall on. Rest in His tender care for you. Receive His peace and strength to carry on each day.

However, hear my heart on this, sometimes our quiet time can become so one-sided that we forget we are talking to El Shaddai; God Almighty. "Ah, Lord God! It is You who have made the heavens and the earth by your great power and by your outstretched arm! Nothing is too hard for You" (Jeremiah 32:17 ESV) He is unlimited in power. Not only does He give power and strength to His people, nothing is too hard for Him.

Jesus is our compassionate High Priest who understands and

cares. He is with us through every detail of our lives and is intimately involved. He experienced life on earth and understands our emotions. He doesn't condemn us or chastise us in our sufferings. He is with us and His eye is on us.

Jesus said, "In this world you will have trouble. But take heart! I have overcome the world." (John 16:33 NIV) We all face problems and concerns that have the potential to strangle peace out of our lives, rob us of joy and cause us to lose heart. Please hear me when I say I am not making light of your problems and concerns. I know they are real. I know they are serious, but I want to encourage you to shift your focus and take heart. How do we shift our focus from ourselves to God more often? We can take a lesson from sparrows.

I love that God mentioned birds in scripture. His Word specifically speaks of sparrows. I wanted to know why. In researching, I found that they protect their nests from intruders by singing. When the sparrow is under attack from an enemy, it sings! Now there's a lesson we can take to our quiet time. He is worthy of our praise. When difficult times surround you, sing praises to God. I can't promise that the difficult times will be removed, but I can promise a change in your heart.

The disciples saw Jesus pray many times. They listened as Jesus poured out His heart and they were compelled to ask Him, "Lord, teach us to pray." The prayer Jesus used to teach His disciples begins with praise, "Our Father in heaven, hallowed be Your name." Praising God is as important as asking God.

When we take the time to meditate about a particular characteristic or quality of God, our eyes shift attention from ourselves and our problems to the greatness and goodness of God. Our focus changes. Our attitudes are adjusted. Our burdens become lighter.

He is worthy of all our praise and He desires our praise. Through our praise, He prepares our hearts for the right perspective to worship and pray. Often times when our hearts are heavy with problems and concerns it is the most difficult time to praise. But in praising Him peace, strength and renewed trust buoy our hearts.

Here are some ideas to help us shift our one-sided focus back to God.

- List concerns one by one and offer the list to your Heavenly Father
- Ask for a grateful heart.
- Read a Psalm a day. Echo the praises found in each one.
- Meditate on a particular attribute of God and write a prayer of thanksgiving in your journal.
- Search for a scripture that praises Him. Write it on an index card and place it in your pocket. Read it often throughout the day as an exclamation of praise.
- Praise Him through nature. Take a walk enjoying all He has created for us thanking Him for everything that captures your attention.
- Have your quiet time outside early one morning or late at night. Be still before Him in holy worship.
- Put away your prayer requests for one day. Praise and thank Him each time you speak to Him from sunrise to sunset.
- Pray with a grateful heart for all He has done, all He is doing, and all He is yet to do.

Father God, I ask for you to help me keep my focus on Your Son, Jesus. He's all I need. He's all I want. Keep me close to You. Forgive me for grumbling and complaining. Fill my heart and mouth with praise for You. You are worthy! I love You. In the precious name of Jesus, amen.

Chapter Nine
Honestly!

"The Lord is near to all who call on Him, to all who call on Him in truth." Psalm 145:18 NIV

When my boys, Dale and Steven, were younger and returned home from school, I would ask them the usual mom question, "How was school?" The usual reply was, "OK". So much for having a meaningful, honest conversation! However, there were days that my heart would soar when they excitedly shared the events of their day with me. "Guess how much I bench-pressed today? Just look at these "guns"! Coach Thompson said...." "I made an 'A' on an art project, want to see it?"

My heart would scream, "Are you kidding me?" "Yes, I want to know how much you bench-pressed!" "Yes, I want to see your artwork!" I wanted them to share their hearts with me. I wanted them to share their joys, their hurts, their concerns, even their random thoughts with me. Why? Because I loved them (still do) and wanted to be involved in their young lives (have to watch that now). I wanted them to come to me with their problems and come to me with their happy thoughts. I wanted to give advice, pray with them, laugh with them, rejoice with them, even cry with them. I delighted in their presence (still do).

Many times they would share things with me that as a mother, I really didn't want to know. However, I am so grateful that they trusted me with their innermost thoughts. Other times, they tried to hide things that would eventually find them out. For instance, we received an envelope in the mail from Steven's middle school. Inside was a form indicating that he had been written up on the bus for misbehaving. My husband and I kept waiting for him to tell us, yet he refused to come clean until we confronted him about it. He was punished for the ticket and for trying to conceal the bus ticket. It would have been easier on him had he simply told us about the ticket when it happened.

God delights in your presence. He desires that we engage in an ongoing conversation with Him about the daily stuff of life. He wants us to share our hearts honestly. Don't worry about "proper" words in prayer. Just talk to Him. Share your hurts, share your sorrows, share your joys, your excitement, your mistakes, share it all freely and honestly. God listens intently in love and compassion.

Often we are ashamed of our honest thoughts and feelings. We think, I'm a Christian, I shouldn't be thinking this or feeling this way, so we try to avoid or hide our true feelings from God, our Creator. We attempt to hide our sin. Pretty silly, isn't it? He is not fooled when we put on our disguises. He knows every thread of every thought, feeling or sin we harbor. He knows us better than we know ourselves!

"For the word of God is living and powerful, and sharper than any two-edged sword, piercing even to the division of soul and spirit, and of joints and marrow, and is a discerner of the thoughts and intents of the heart. And there is no creature hidden from His sight, but all things are naked and open to the eyes of Him to whom we must give account." (Hebrews 4:12,13 NKJV) We simply cannot hide our true thoughts and true motives from God. He knows!

Truth in the original Greek Language means, not concealing. The beauty of being honest with God is that it leads to repentance. Repentance leads to forgiveness. Withholding honesty from God is an obstacle to intimacy in our relationship with Him. When I finally get real with God, He moves in a mighty way to change my heart. Close friends share honesty and openness. That's what He wants from us.

Somehow we have gotten the idea that our prayers must always be pleasant and polite. The Bible is full of examples of God's people pouring out raw honesty from the depths of their hearts. No dancing around the issues, just honest hearts before

God in prayer. Read the Book of Psalms for example after example of these prayers.

God listens when we pray in eloquence or brokenhearted weariness. He listens when we pray full of hopeful anticipation or in our feelings of hopelessness. The one thing He desires is honesty.

David was a man after God's own heart. He expressed his feelings and emotions freely with God. How? He prayed from his heart. Read Psalm 13 which is just one example of David praying through a difficult time as he wrestled with his thoughts and emotions.

Exhaustion, physical illness and suffering can cause our emotions to go haywire. Our pride, anger and selfishness can cause us to view people and situations incorrectly. Prayer is the best place to reveal our true feelings. Honesty in prayer is a safeguard against acting on your feelings.

In the Garden of Gethsemane (Matthew 26:36-46), Jesus prayed honestly that God would take away His cup of suffering He was about to experience on the cross. He knew He would find mercy not punishment, comfort not reproach. Jesus waited until He submitted to the Father's will before departing from the garden. What if He hadn't? He had that choice. He chose you and me.

If you are not familiar with Job, read Chapters one and two. Job was honest with God during his suffering. He and his friends looked and looked for a logical explanation and reason for his suffering. Instead of answers to his "why" questions, Job discovered something far greater; the majesty of his Creator was revealed to him. In honest conversation with God, our questions can be replaced by an overwhelming awareness of God's loving presence.

God allows us to express our true feelings in prayer. He responds with mercy and compassion. We need to be willing to allow God to bring our emotions in line with His Truth and perfect will before we move forward in any issue. As a result of honesty in prayer, we will find a deeper and more intimate relationship with God through Jesus Christ. What do you need to honestly talk to Him about? Is there something you've been trying to conceal? Lay your heart bare and spread it out before God in prayer. Use a Bible concordance or Topical Bible and search for scriptures that speak the Truth to the issue or problem with which you are struggling. Record these scriptures in your journal and pray them back to God. Pray for your heart to align with His Truth and will.

Father God, I confess that I have been trying to hide _____ from You. It seems so silly to admit that I could possibly hide anything from You. I ask for You to forgive me. I want to be totally honest with You about what I think and what I feel now. (Take time now to pray honestly) I know my thoughts/actions are wrong. I ask that You reveal Your Truth to me and help me submit to Your perfect will in this situation. I want to honor You. Thank You, Father, that I can be honest with You and You respond in love, mercy and Truth. In the mighty name of Jesus, amen.

Chapter Ten
Not Another Prayer Request!

"Therefore confess your sins to each other and pray for each other so that you may be healed. The prayer of a righteous person is powerful and effective." James 5:16 (NIV)

I'm sure you've heard the expression, "Prayer Warrior"; those who are committed to praying for others. God has gifted them with a desire to pray for the things that I believe are on His heart. I believe He has gifted them with faith to pray boldly for others and for the needs around the world. He gives special insight into the spiritual battles raging all around. Maybe you are a Prayer Warrior. Even if you don't find yourself in the same category, we are all called to pray.

My quiet time often includes time to pray for others. Early on, I became overwhelmed with prayer requests. I would worry that I had forgotten to pray for someone who had asked. Other times I became frustrated and distressed at the number of requests. Admittedly I've thought to myself, "Not another prayer request!". Nope, not proud of that but it's true. It is a privilege and an honor to pray for others and to be involved in what God is doing in the lives of others.

This is a system I developed that works for me and maybe it will help you too. First of all, when someone asks me to pray for their specific need, I ask if we can pray together at that moment. It's fresh on our hearts and minds. Other times when that is not feasible, I write the request down on anything handy or in the "Notes" on my phone.

A 5 X 7 ring-bound notebook saved my prayer life. I divided the notebook into seven sections. One for each day. Monday is the day set aside to pray for my family. Tuesday is designated for my friends. Wednesday is set aside to pray for others, some I know, some I don't. Thursday prayer time is for our country. Friday's prayer focus is for the world and the Deaf which are dear to my heart. Saturday's prayers are for salvation for the lost and Sunday's prayer time is devoted to my church and churches in general.

Those prayer requests written on scraps of paper or in my phone are transferred to my Prayer Notebook in the appropriate category. This is just a system to help me organize my prayer life but that doesn't mean if someone asks me to pray for their brother to receive salvation, I can't pray for that until Saturday. Of course, I'll pray as soon as I can but will write that request down to pray for again.

When requests are answered it is crossed off my list. But frankly, we don't always know the outcome of our prayers. That's not our job, it can be our delight, but not our job. That belongs to God.

Often scripture will come to mind as I'm praying for someone. I write it along with their name in my prayer notebook. Whatever your method, don't fail to pray for someone who has asked. I'm reminded of what the prophet Samuel said in 1 Samuel 12:23 "As for me, far be it from me that I should sin against the Lord by failing to pray for you." (NIV)

Here are some thoughts and ways my friends keep up with their prayer requests:

Sonja uses a book that looks like a journal. She also puts separate pieces of paper in the book since she jots the requests on whatever is available also. She says her book gets pretty messy because she doesn't organize it like she used to. She puts the requests all together.

Sue writes her requests on index cards and reviews the list during her prayer time. When God responds, she crosses out the request. When one card is filled, she starts a new one. She records the request and God's answer in her journal. She dates the entry. When she is praying for the sick, she includes all people who are suffering from that disease. That stays on the card indefinitely because she doesn't know specifically who she is praying for.

I asked MaryKay for her thoughts and here is her response in her own words:

"Perhaps I think of prayer in too elementary or juvenile of terms, but I truly just see it as a conversation with God. So, for me, that conversation is on-going throughout the day (and sometimes throughout the night too. God determines that). God began to develop my conversation-relationship with Him years ago; it was so gradual that I really can't pinpoint it. However, as what tends to happen with <u>all</u> relationships, there have been some defining moments, moments that almost take my breath away because I can feel God so extremely close that I envision us walking hand and hand through the prayer-needed moments.

In 2012 I began to journal those moments. (I wish I had begun doing that earlier.) The journaling not only keeps my prayers organized, it is the <u>most</u> important piece of my prayer journey – it helps me <u>remember.</u> Remembering that God's ways and thoughts are higher than mine, that He is unchanging, that He is who He says He is – the same trustworthy God who always carries out to completion the good works He has begun, and He is working around me ALL the time - <u>that</u> is whom I'm having prayer conversations with!

Early on in my prayer ministry days I would feel extremely <u>burdened</u> at times because of the sheer weight of carrying all those prayer petitions. God has since taught me that He <u>never</u> asks me to carry the weight of them. I am just the vessel He has chosen to be the intercessor. No more, no less. And so, with Philippians 4:6-7 6 "Do not be anxious about anything, but in every situation, by prayer and petition, with thanksgiving, present your requests to God. 7 And the peace of God, which transcends all understanding, will guard your hearts and your minds in Christ Jesus." (NIV) in mind, the conversations with God continue throughout the day.

How do I organize those prayer petitions? First, if someone asks me to pray for them, I try my hardest to pause during the day and take care of doing that right then and there. Relying on the truth of Matthew 18:20 *"For where two or three gather in my name, there am I with them."* *(NIV)* I ask the person if they will go to the Throne of Mercy and Grace <u>with</u> me in that moment. Then I don't have the worry of <u>forgetting</u> to intercede on behalf of my friend, when that request has been presented to me in an often-rushed world. If we are not able to address the request right then, I will jot it down on whatever is most convenient – in my Notes on my iPhone, in my planning calendar, or in the notebook I keep in my pocketbook. The key is to <u>not</u> forget, which I would be apt to do. When I say, "I am praying for you", I mean it most sincerely. When time allows, I then transfer those petitions into my journal.

Of course, the prayer requests don't always come from an external source; sometimes God just interrupts my day to bring someone to mind. Based on experience, I know that I must stop whatever I am doing so that I might be still before Him, standing in the gap for that "someone" He has just brought to my mind. And although I don't know specific prayer petitions in that moment, I lift the person to Jehovah and ask for His favor over them.

Those are the ways I keep track of prayer petitions; of course, I think it is very personal to the person. I'm sure there are many ways; these ways work best for me.

Today, when I skim over my journal that is organized by date, I can see that it was 5 years ago God had placed a young church member on my heart to lift in intercessory prayer. But that wasn't all. He also asked me to serve her. It is such an amazing honor when God invites me into His work! As I glance through those 5-year-old petitions I'm again reminded this morning, as I enter into my quiet time with the One who holds <u>all</u> petitions, that He walked hand-in-hand with me then. He will do the same with me today, as we continue our conversation in prayer. I remember."

When someone asks you to pray for them, be sure to do so. Find a method to record prayer requests that works for you. More importantly, you may not remember. Trying to keep those all in your head will probably make your eyes crossed.

Lord, Help me be diligent in praying for others. Cross my path with people who need you and need prayer and allow me the privilege of praying for them. Help me find a way to be faithful in praying for others. Thank You for the opportunity and privilege to bring them to You in prayer.
In the mighty name of Jesus. amen

Conclusion

Sweet child of God, the devil certainly doesn't want us to spend time with God and will do anything to interfere. He would love for us to throw up our hands and give up because he knows the more time we spend with Jesus, the more we will know Him and be transformed into His image. The enemy of our souls will do anything to keep us from becoming more like Jesus and destroy our effective witness for Him. However, we can't blame everything on our enemy, sometimes we simply lack discipline. Many things threaten to rob us of this precious time. Press through and refuse to give up! Place a high value on spending time with the lover of your soul, Jesus.

Your spiritual life depends on it.

God is calling you to lay aside the worries of your day.
To quiet your busy mind and
find a hiding place,
a quiet place
to be still and listen.

"Those who live in the shelter of the Most High will find rest in the shadow of the Almighty. This I declare about the Lord: He alone is my refuge, my place of safety; he is my God, and I trust him. For he will rescue you from every trap and protect you from deadly disease. He will cover you with his feathers. He will shelter you with his wings. His faithful promises are your armor and protection." Psalm 91:1-4 (NLT)

Made in the USA
Columbia, SC
11 April 2021